SCORPIO TRAINING

KETTLEBELL EXERCISES

WWW.DROGASKORPIONA.COM

Title: Scorpio training. Kettlebell Exercises.
Author: Marcin Majchrzak
Cover artwork: Marcin Majchrzak

MM EUROBOOKS

Edition I

Poznań 2020

For Andriana

TABLE OF CONTENTS

WARNING 1

GENERAL TRAINING TIPS.. 2

WARM UP 3

CHEST 17

SHOULDERS 28

ABS 35

LEGS 42

BACK 57

BICEPS 62

TRICEPS 70

FOREARMS 76

FULL BODY WORKOUT 82

WARNING

Before beginning training, consult a physician, physiotherapist and qualified personal trainer to rule out any contraindications.

Exemplary exercises are presented for healthy people, and their performance may be inappropriate for people after injuries, with some diseases or problems with the musculoskeletal system or other ailments.

Exercises presented in this publication should be performed only under the supervision of an experienced and qualified personal trainer.

All information provided in this publication is of general informational and educational nature, may not be treated as medical advice, and the use of the information contained is at your own risk.

The author has made every effort to ensure that this product is fully valuable, but is not responsible for how this knowledge will be used and for potential consequences.

GENERAL TRAINING TIPS

1. Before beginning physical training, consult a physician, physiotherapist and qualified personal trainer to rule out any contraindications.

2. Warm up before training by combining cardio exercises with specific body parts. This will reduce the risk of injury and also ensure the full effectiveness of muscle work.

3. Finish your workout gently by doing reduced-intensity cardio and stretching exercises.

4. Specify the training goal and adjust the duration of the training unit and the load applied to it. Beginners should choose a weight that will allow free control and thus shape the right habits and the right technique.

5. Start the training unit from the starting position. The weight lies in front of you, and your position is characterized by a slight knee deflection, an upright position and loose shoulders and arms. Raising the weight precedes the knees bending and torso inclination, but keeping the straight back. As the position is straight, the chest should be pushed out and the shoulders removed.

6. Take care of the correct technique. This ensures obtaining the expected results and the safety of the exercises performed. Training should take place under the guidance of a qualified instructor who will correct any errors.

When starting most of the exercises, you should keep an eye on your straight back, retracted abdomen and unstretched chest, as well as your shoulder blades pulled back and down, but this is not the rule for all exercises! Each training should take place under the supervision of a personal trainer!

7. Changes introduced to our training plan protect against stagnation and guarantee its effectiveness.

8. Ensure proper breathing while exercising, which increases their effectiveness. In practice, this means breathing out at the moment of the greatest muscle tension. Translating this into specific groups of exercises, exhale while squeezing the weight or pushing the hips and throwing the weight forward. Inhale characterizes the phase of lowering the weight and swing to each other.

9. Give your body time to recover between training units.

WARM UP

1. CARDIO

JUMP ROPE

JUMPING JACKS

BOXING RUN

2. NECK
EAR TO SHOULDER

LEFT / RIGHT

UP / DOWN

3.   SHOULDERS
FORWARD / BACK CIRCULATION

LEFT FORWARD / RIGHT BACK CIRCULATION

CHEST RACKS

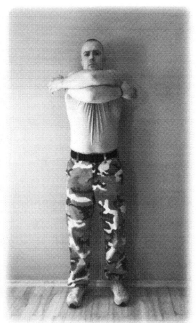

SHRUGS FRONT / BACK

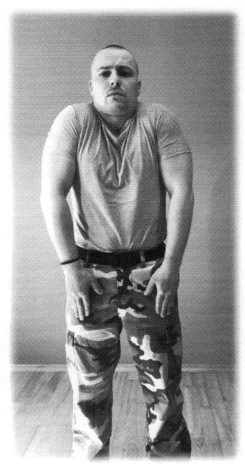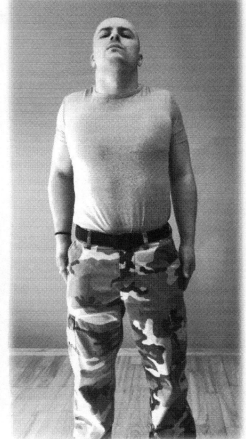

4. BACK
ROTATION

SIDES

CHEST OPENING

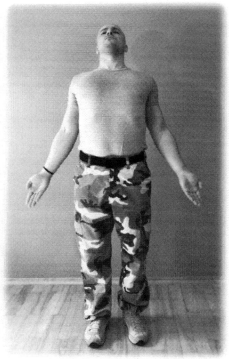

5. ELBOWS
STRAIGHTENING

6. WRISTS
WRISTS ROTATION

 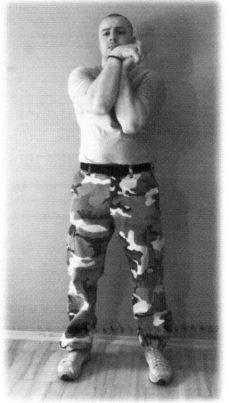

7. HIPS
ROTATION

SIDES

FRONT / BACK

CIRCULATION

FRONT / BACK SWINGS

SIDE SWING

8. KNEES
FRONT / BACK SWING

HEELS FOR BUTTOCKS

9.   CUBES
CIRCULATION

ROLLING INSIDE / OUTSIDE

STRETCHING FRONT / BACK

10. NO WEIGHT EXCERCISES

CHEST

ONE-HAND PRESS
LEVEL: MEDIUM
EQUIPMENT: KETTLEBELL
TARGET: CHEST
INSTRUCTION:
1. HOLD THE WEIGHT IN ONE HAND AND LAY ON THE FLOOR, WHEN THE SECOND HAND IS BASED ON THE GROUND
2. LIFT THE WEIGHT UP WITH ROTATION OF THE WRIST AT THE SAME TIME
3. SLOWLY LOWER THE WEIGHT TO THE START POSITION

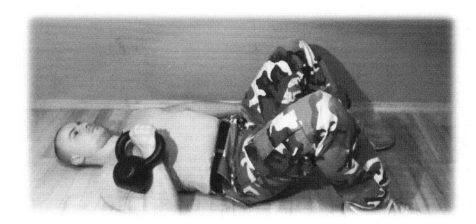

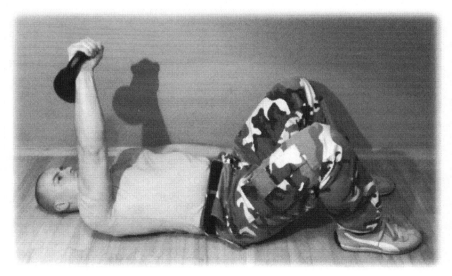

PUSH UP

LEVEL: EASY

EQUIPMENT: 2 X KETTLEBELL

TARGET: CHEST, TRICPES, CORE

INSTRUCTION:

1. PLACE KETTLEBELL AT SHOULDER HEIGHT
2. GRAB WEIGHTS AND TAKE PUSH UP POSITION - EXTENDED LEGS, FOOT TOES AND STRAIGHT BACK
3. LOW DOWN THE POSITION AND RETURN TO THE START POSITION DYNAMICALLY

FLOOR PUSHING

LEVEL: EASY

EQUIPMENT: KETTLEBELL

TARGET: CHEST, TRICPES

INSTRUCTION:

1. LAY DOWN ON THE FLOOR
2. TAKE THE KETTLEBELL IN BOTH HANDS AND LIFT ABOVE THE CHEST
3. SLOWLY LOW THE WEIGHT, LEADING THE ELBOWS ALONG THE BODY
4. STOP KETTLEBELL ABOVE THE CHEST AND DYNAMICALLY STRAIGHT YOUR HANDS UP

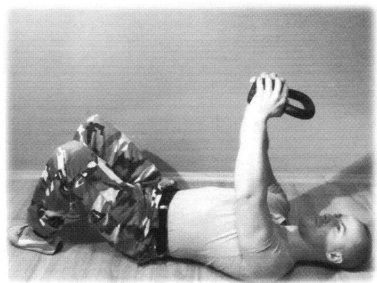

STANDING PRESS

LEVEL: EASY

EQUIPMENT: KETTLEBELL

TARGET: CHEST, SHOULDERS

INSTRUCTION:

1. STAND WITH LEGS LIGHTLY BENDED

2. GRIP KETTLEBELL IN BOTH HANDS - CLOSE TO THE CHEST, ELBOWS NEAR THE BODY

3. PUSH THE WEIGHT IN FORNT OF YOU

4. BACK TO THE START POSITION

 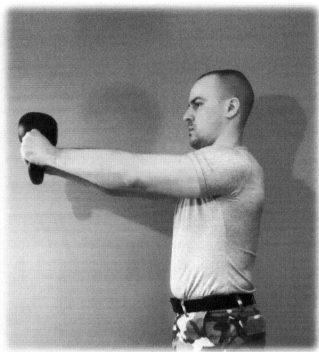

DECLINE FLOOR PUSH

LEVEL: MEDIUM

EQUIPMENT: KETTLEBELL

TARGET: CHEST

INSTRUCTION:

1. LAY ON THE FLOOR, BEND THE KNEES AND PUSH THE HIPS TO BRIDGE POSITION
2. GRIP KETTLEBELL IN BOTH HANDS, CLOSE TO THE CHEST, ELBOWS NEAR THE BODY
3. PUSH THE KETTLEBELL UP
4. BACK TO THE START POSITION

FLOOR BOTH HANDS PRESS

LEVEL: EASY

EQUIPMENT: 2 X KETTLEBELL

TARGET: CHEST, SHOULDERS

INSTRUCTION:

1. LAY ON THE FLOOR, SHOULDERS TO THE GROUND, LEGS BENDED

2. . GRIP KETTLEBELLS IN YOUR HAND WITH THE RIGHT ANGLE OF THE ELBOWS AND TRICEPS ON THE GROUND

3. PUSH WEIGHTS SO YOUR HANDS MEET AT THECHEST HEIGHT

4. BACK TO THE START POSITION

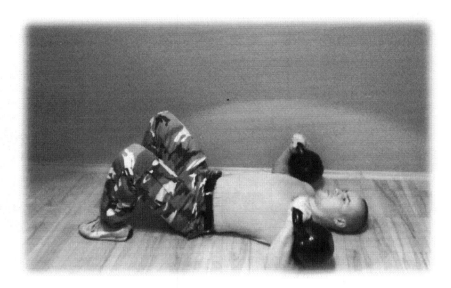

DECLINE BOTH HANDS PRESS

LEVEL: MEDIUM

EQUIPMENT: 2 X KETTLEBELL

TARGET: CHEST, SHOULDERS

INSTRUCTION:

1. LAY ON THE FLOOR, BEND THE KNEES AND PUSH THE HIP TO CREATE A BRIDGE POSITION

2. GRIP KETTLEBELLS IN YOUR HAND WITH THE RIGHT ANGLE OF THE ELBOWS AND TRICEPS ON THE GROUND

3. PUSH WEIGHTS SO YOUR HANDS MEET AT THECHEST HEIGHT

4. BACK TO THE START POSITION

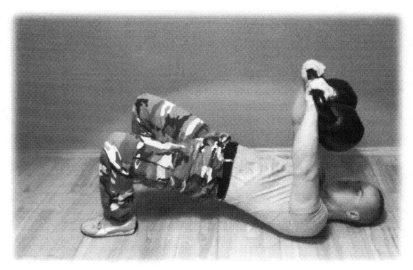

CROSS PRESS

LEVEL: EASY

EQUIPMENT: 2 X KETTLEBELL

TARGET: CHEST

INSTRUCTION:

1. LAY ON THE FLOOR WITH SHOULDERS ON THE GROUN

2. TAEK KETTLEBELLS IN YOUR HAND

3. PRESS WEIGHTS INSIDE THAT HANDS MEET AT THE CHEST HEIGHT

4. BACK TO THE START POSITION

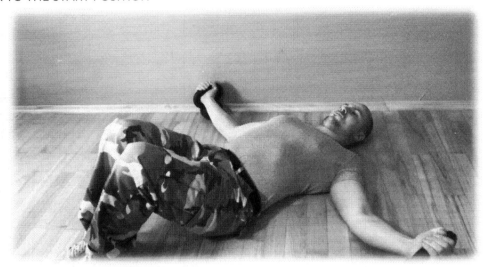

UP PUSH

LEVEL: EASY

EQUIPMENT: KETTLEBELL

TARGET: CHEST, SHOULDERS

INSTRUCTION:

1. STAND TALL, LEGS LIGHTLY BENDED

2. GRIP KETTLEBELL IN BOTH HANDS, CLOSE TO THE CHEST, ELBOWS NEAR THE BODY

3. PUSH THE WEIGHT IN FONT OF YOU AND UP

4. BACK TO THE START POSITION

DECLINE PLEXUS PRESS

LEVEL: MEDIUM

EQUIPMENT: 2 X KETTLEBELL

TARGET: CHEST

INSTRUCTION:

1. LAY ON THE FLOOR, SHOULDERS ON THE GROUND

2. BEND THE KNEES AND PUSH THE HIP TO THE BRIDGE POSITION

3. GRIP KETTLEBELLS IN YOUR HAND

4. PRESS KETTLEBELLS INSIDE THAT HANDS MEET AT CHEST HEIGHT

PUSH UP WITH ROWING

LEVEL: MEDIUM

EQUIPMENT: 2 X KETTLEBELL

TARGET: CHEST, BACK

INSTRUCTION:

1. PLACE WEIGHT WEIGHT AT SHOULDER HEIGHT
2. GRAIN WEIGHTS AND TAKE POSITION FOR PUMPS - EXTENDED LEGS, FOOT TOES AND STRAIGHT BACK
3. LOWER ITEM CONTROLLED AND DYNAMIC MOTION RETURN TO THE END POSITION
4. PULL THE WEIGHT CLOSE TO THE BODY
5. REPEAT ON THE OTHER SIDE

SHOULDERS

ONE ARM UP PRESS
LEVEL: EASY
EQUIPMENT: KETTLEBELL
TARGET: SHOULDER MUSCLES
INSTRUCTION:
1. GRAB THE KETTLEBELL IN ONE HAND
2. PRESS WEIGHT ABOVE THE HEAD, ROTATING THE WRIST
3. RETURN TO THE START POSITION

SHRUGS

LEVEL: EASY

EQUIPMENT: 2 X KETTLEBELL

TARGET: QUAD SIDE MUSCLES

INSTRUCTION:

1. STAND UP AND GRIP KETTLEBELLS ON BOTH SIDES

2. RAISE YOUR SHOULDER TO THE EARS

3. PAUSE TENTION AT THE FINAL MOVEMENT PHASE

4. BACK TO THE START POSITION

SIDE RISE

LEVEL: EASY

EQUIPMENT: 2 X KETTLEBELL

TARGET: SHOULDER MUSCLES, BREAST MUSCLES, QUAD SIDE MUSCLES

INSTRUCTION:

1. GRAB KETTLEBELLS AND STAND TALL
2. PULL THE SHOULDERS BACK
3. RAISE THE KETTLE UP, CREATING THE CROSS
4. BACK TO THE START POSITION

ONE HAND CHIN PULL

LEVEL: EASY

EQUIPMENT: KETTLEBELL

TARGET: SHOULDER MUSCLES, QUADSULAR MUSCLES

INSTRUCTION:

1. GRAB THE KETTLEBELL IN ONE HAND
2. PULL THE WEIGHT ALONG THE BODY UP TO THE CHIN, WITH THE ELBOW PROJECTING OUTSIDE
3. BACK TO THE START POSITION

HALO

LEVEL: EASY

EQUIPMENT: KETTLEBELL

TARGET: SHOULDER MUSCLES

INSTRUCTION:

1. GRIP THE KETTLEBELL IN BOTH HANDS

2. SET THE KETTLEBELL NEAR THE CHEST

3. PERFORM ROUND MOVE AROUND THE HEAD WITH A SMOOTH MOTION

4. GO BACK TO THE START POSITION AND REPEAT CHANGING THE DIRECTION

SIDE PRESS

LEVEL: EASY
EQUIPMENT: 2 X KETTLEBELL
TARGET: SHOULDER MUSCLES
INSTRUCTION:
1. GRIP KETTLEBELLS IN BOTH HANDS
2. SET THEM DOWN NEXT TO EACH OTHER
3. REMEMBER ABOUT STRAIGHT BACK
4. PRESS WEIGHTS ASIDE
5. BACK TO THE START POSITION

TURKISH GET UP

LEVEL: DIFFICULT

EQUIPMENT: KETTLEBELL

TARGET: SHOULDERS, LEGS, ARMS

INSTRUCTION:

1. LAY ON THE FLOOR, GET THE KETTLEBELL PUSH IT UP

2. TAKE POSITION TO SIT

3. STAND UP, ALL THE TIME MAINTAINING THE WEIGHT ABOVE THE HEAD

4. LAY DOWN, MOVING IN REVERSE ORDER

ABS

TWISTS
LEVEL: MEDIUM
EQUIPMENT: KETTLEBELL
TARGET: ABS
INSTRUCTION:
1. SIT DOWN ON THE FLOOR WITH STRAIGHT LEGS
2. TAKE THE KETTLEBELL IN BOTH HANDS AND LIFT UP TO THE CHEST
3. RAISE YOUR LEGS SO THEY DO NOT TOUCH THE GROUND AND KEEP THE BALANCE
4. PERFORM THE BODY ROTATION BY MOVING THE WEIGHT FOR THE LEG LINE -
ONCE FROM THE LEFT, ONCE FROM THE RIGHT

UP RISES
LEVEL: EASY
EQUIPMENT: KETTLEBELL
TARGET: ABS
INSTRUCTION:
1. LAY ON THE EARTH WITH YOUR LEGS UP
2. GRAB THE WEIGHT AND KEEP IT NEAR THE CHEST
3. LIFT THE BODY AND PUSH THE WEIGHT TOWARDS YOUR FEET
4. BACK TO LOWER POSITION, DO NOT TOUCH THE GROUND WITH SHOULDERS

BENDING ABOVE THE HEAD

LEVEL: EASY

EQUIPMENT: KETTLEBELL

TARGET: ANGLES MUSCLES

INSTRUCTION:

1. STAND STRAIGHT AND LIFT THE KETTLEBELL ABOVE YOUR HEAD

2. BEND THE BODY TO THE SIDE WITH STRAIGHT HANDS

3. BACK TO THE START POSITION AND REPEAT ON THE OTHER SIDE

RISES

LEVEL: EASY

EQUIPMENT: KETTLEBELL

TARGET: ABS

INSTRUCTION:

1. LAY ON THE FLOOR WITH BENDED LEGS

2. GRAB THE WEIGHT AND KEEP IT NEAR THE CHEST

3. LIFT THE BODY AND PUSH THE KETTLEBELL

4. BACK TO THE START POSITION, DO NOT TOUCH THE GROUND WITH SHOULDERS

WINDMILL

LEVEL: MEDIUM

EQUIPMENT: KETTLEBELL

TARGET: ANGLES MUSCLES

INSTRUCTION:

1. STAND TALL

2. LIFT THE WEIGHT WITH ONE HAND OVER THE HEAD

3. MAKE A BEND AND TOUCH THE FOOT WITH YOUR FREE HAND

4. KEEP STRAIGHT BACK AND LEGS, THE HAND ABOVE THE HEAD DOES NOT CHANGE THE POSITION

SIDE BEND

LEVEL: EASY

EQUIPMENT: KETTLEBELL

TARGET: ANGLES MUSCLES

INSTRUCTION:

1. STAND STRAIGHT AND GRAB WEIGHT FROM ONE SIDE OF THE BODY

2. THE SECOND HAND STILL AT THE HEAD

3. PERFORM A BEND TO THE KETTLEBELL SIDE

4. BACK TO THE START POSITION AND CHANGE SIDE

PASSING BETWEEN LEGS

LEVEL: DIFFICULT

EQUIPMENT: KETTLEBELL

TARGET: ABS

INSTRUCTION:

1. SIT ON THE FLOOR AND LIFT YOUR LEGS
2. GRAB THE KETTLEBELL ON THE ONE SIDE
3. PASS THE KETTLEBELL TO THE SECOND HAND UNDER THE LEG BY LIFTING IT AT THE SAME TIME
4. REPEAT ON THE OTHER SIDE

LEGS

SWING

LEVEL: EASY
EQUIPMENT: KETTLEBELL
TARGET: BUTTOCKS, SQUARE, CALVES
INSTRUCTION:
1. STAND UP, STRAIGHT BACK, BENDED KNEES
2. BEND AND GRIP THE KETTLEBELL IN BOTH HANDS
3. PULL THE KETTLEBELL BETWEEN YOUR LEGS
4. DYNAMICLY PUSH THE HIPS FORWARD

STEP AND PASS

LEVEL: MEDIUM
EQUIPMENT: KETTLEBELL
TARGET: BUTTOCKS, CALVES
INSTRUCTION:
1. STAND UP WITH STRAIGHT BACK
2. GRIP THE KETTLEBELL IN YOUR HAND
3. MAKE A STEP, BEND KNEE - 90 DEGREES AND HOLD BACK STRAIGHT
4. PASS THE WEIGHT UNDER THE BENDED LEG WITH
5. BACK TO THE START POSITION AND EXECUTE TO THE OTHER PAGE

DEADLIFT

LEVEL: EASY

EQUIPMENT: KETTLEBELL

WORK: BUTTOCKS, HAMSTRINGS, UPPER FRONT

INSTRUCTION:

1. STAND TALL WITH STRAIGHT BACK AND THE PULLED SHOULDERS

2. GRAP THE KETTLEBELL IN BOTH HANDS

3. BEND THE POSITION WITH STRAIGHT BACK - THE HEAD IS AN EXTENSION OF THE SPINE AND THE WEIGHT IS RUNNING AS CLOSE TO THE BODY AS POSSIBLE

4. BACK TO THE START POSITION WHILE PUSHING THE CHEST OUT

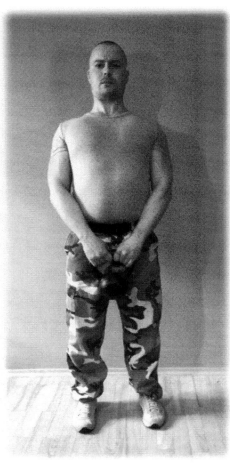

KNEELING SQUAT

LEVEL: EASY

EQUIPMENT: 2 X KETTLEBELL

TARGET: BUTTOCKS, UPPER FRONT

INSTRUCTION:

1. KNEEL WITH STRAIGHT BACK AND FEET BASED ON THE FLOOR WITH THE FINGERS STRAIGHT

2. GRAB KETTLEBELLS AND KEEP NEAR THE CHEST

3. LOWER YOUR POSITION, TOUCHING YOUR HEELS

4. BACK TO THE START POSITION

LEG PUSH

LEVEL: EASY

EQUIPMENT: KETTLEBELL

WORK: FRONT LEG MUSCLES

INSTRUCTION:

1. SIT ON THE CHAIR WITH STRAIGHT BACK

2. PUT THE FOOT UNDER THE KETTLEBELL HANDLE AND PUSH THE LEG

3. BRING THE FOOT BACK AND REPEAT

ONE LEG KNEELING SQUAT

LEVEL: EASY

EQUIPMENT: KETTLEBELL

TARGET: BUTTOCKS, FRONT AND BACK LEG MUSCLES

INSTRUCTION:

1. KNEEL WITH STRAIGHT BACK

2. GRAB THE KETTLEBELL AND KEEP NEAR THE CHEST

3. TAKE A STEP WITH ONE FOOT AND ADD THE OTHER LEG

4. THE BODY DOES NOT CHANGE THE POSITION, THE KNEES- ANGLE OF 90 DEGREES

5. BACK TO THE START POSITION

SUMO SQUAT

LEVEL: EASY

EQUIPMENT: KETTLEBELL

TARGET: BUTTOCKS, FRONT LEG MUSCLES

INSTRUCTION:

1. STAND UP AND GRAB THE KETTLEBELL IN BOTH HANDS
2. KEEP THE KETTLEBELL AND MAKE A DEEP SQUAT
3. BACK TO THE START POSITION AND REPEAT

BRIDGE

LEVEL: MEDIUM

EQUIPMENT: KETTLEBELL

TARGET: BUTTOCKS

INSTRUCTION:

1.LIE DOWN WITH BENDED KNEES

2. KEEP THE KETTLEBELL ON YOUR PELVIS

3. PUSH THE HIP TO THE BRIDGE POSITION

4. BACK TO THE START POSITION

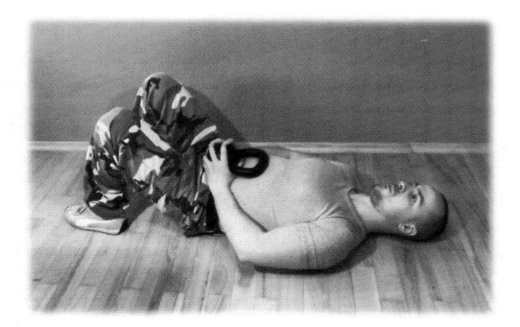

GET UP SQUAT

LEVEL: EASY

EQUIPMENT: KETTLEBELL

TARGET: BUTTOCKS, FRONT LEG MUSCLES

INSTRUCTION:

1. KNEEL WITH STRAIGHT BACK
2. GRAB THE KETTLEBELL AND KEEP NEAR THE CHEST
3. TAKE A STEP THAN ADD THE OTHER LEG AND STAN UP
4. KNEEL ON THE ONE LEG AND BACK TO THE START POSITION

SUMO PULL

LEVEL: EASY

EQUIPMENT: KETTLEBELL

TARGET: BUTTOCKS, FRONT LEG MUSCLES, SHOULDERS

INSTRUCTION:

1. STAND UP AND GRAB THE KETTLEBELL IN BOTH HANDS

2. KEEP THE KETTLEBELL IN FRONT OF YOU AND MAKE A DEEP SQUAT

3. BACK TO THE START POSITION

4. PULL THE WEIGHT ALONG THE BODY UP TO THE CHIN

SIDE STEP

LEVEL: EASY

EQUIPMENT: KETTLEBELL

TARGET: BUTTOCKS, FRONT LEG MUSCLES

INSTRUCTION:

1. STAND STRAIGHT AND GRAB THE KETTLEBELL IN BOTH HANDS

2. KEEP THE KETTLEBELL NEAR THE CHEST AND TAKE A STEP TO THE SIDE

3. GO BACK TO START POSITION AND REPEAT ON THE OTHER SIDE

DOUBLE KETTLEBELL SQUAT

LEVEL: EASY

EQUIPMENT: 2 X KETTLEBELL

TARGET: BUTTOCKS, FRONT LEG MUSCLES

INSTRUCTION:

1. STAND STRAIGHT AND GRAB THE KETTLEBELL IN BOTH HANDS
2. KEEP KETTLEBELLS NEAR THE CHEST
3. KEEP THE BACK STRAIGHT AND DO A SQUAT
4. BACK TO THE START POSITION

KETTLEBELL SQUAT

LEVEL: EASY

EQUIPMENT: KETTLEBELL

TARGET: BUTTOCKS, FRONT LEG MUSCLES

INSTRUCTION:

1. STAND STRAIGHT AND GRAM THE KETTLEBELL IN BOTHHANDS NEAR THE CHEST

2. TAKE A DEEP SQUAT, KEEP YOUR BACK STRAIGHT

3. BACK TO THE START POSITION

ONE LEG BRIDGE
LEVEL: MEDIUM
EQUIPMENT: KETTLEBELL
TARGET:THE BUTTOCKS
INSTRUCTION:
1. LAY ON THE FLOOR WITH HEELS ON THE GROUND
2. BEND THE KNEES AND THE KETTLEBELL ON THE PELVIS
3. PUSH THE HIP TO THE BRIDGE POSITION
4. BACK TO THE START POSITION

NARROW SQUAT

LEVEL: EASY

EQUIPMENT: KETTLEBELL

TARGET: BUTTOCKS, FRONT LEG MUSCLES

INSTRUCTION:

1. STAND TALL WITH FEET NEAR EACH OTHER
2. GRAB THE KETTLEBELL NEAR YOUR CHEST
3. DO A DEEP SQUAT
4. BACK TO THE START POSITION

BACK

KETTLEBELL TRANSFER
LEVEL: MEDIUM
EQUIPMENT: KETTLEBELL
TARGET: BACK, CHEST
INSTRUCTION:
1. LIE ON THE FLOOR AND BEND YOUE KNEES
2. GRAB THE KETTLEBELL WITH BOTH HANDS AND LIFT UPON YOUR CHEST
3. MOVE THE KETTLEBELL BEHIND YOUR HEAD
4. BACK TO THE START POSITION

KETTLEBELL ROW

LEVEL: MEDIUM
EQUIPMENT: 2 X KETTLEBELL
TARGET: BACK, SHOULDERS, BICEPS
INSTRUCTION:
1. STAND STRAIGHT, GRAB KETTLEBELLS AND BEND THE POSITION
2. KEEP KETTLEBELLS IN FORNT OF YOU AND KEEP THE STRAIGHT BACK
3. PULL KETTLEBELLS UP WITH ELBOWS NEAR THE BODY
4. PAUSE THE MOVE AND REPEAT

SINGLE ROW

LEVEL: MEDIUM

EQUIPMENT: KETTLEBELL

TARGET: BACK, SHOULDERS, BICEPS

INSTRUCTION:

1. STAND STRAIGHT, AND BEND THE POSITION
2. GRAB THE KETTLEBELL AND KEEP THE BACK STRAIGHT
3. FREE HAND BASED ON THE KNEE
4. PULL THE KETTLEBELL UP WITH ELBOW NEAR THE BODY
5. MAKE A PAUSE AND REPEAT

ALTERNATIVE ROW

LEVEL: MEDIUM

EQUIPMENT: 2 X KETTLEBELL

TARGET: BACK, SHOULDERS, BICEPS

INSTRUCTION:

1. STAND STRAIGHT AND BEND THE POSITION

2. GRAB KETTLEBELLS AND KEEP THE STRAIGHT BACK

3. PULL THE KETTLEBELL WITH ONE HAND, ELBOW NEAR THE BODY

4. PERFORM PAUSE AND REPEAT WITH THE OTHER HAND

GROUND ROW

LEVEL: MEDIUM

EQUIPMENT: 2 X KETTLEBELL

TARGET: BACK, SHOULDER, BICEPS, CORE

INSTRUCTION:

1. TAKE A PUSH UP POSITION

2. GRAB KETTLEBELLS - EXTENDED LEGS, FOOT, TOES AND BACK STRAIGHT

3. PULL KETTLEBELL UP WITH ELBOW NEAR THE BODY

4. MAKE A PAUSE AND BACK TO THE PUSHU UP POSITION

5. REPEAT ON THE OTHER SIDE

BICEPS

BENDING ARMS
LEVEL: EASY
EQUIPMENT: 2 X KETTLEBELL
TARGER: BICEPS, SHOULDERS
INSTRUCTION:
1. STAND STRAIGHT AND GRAB KETTLEBELLS
2. BEND THE ELBOWS
3. BACK TO THE START POSITION

WIDE ARM BENDING

LEVEL: EASY

EQUIPMENT: 2 X KETTLEBELL

TARGET: BICEPS

INSTRUCTION:

1. STAND STRAIGHT AND GRAB KETTLEBELLS
2. BEND YOUR ELBOWS AND WIDELY RAISE KETTLEBELLS UP
3. BACK TO THE START POSITION

MUG PRESS
LEVEL: EASY
EQUIPMENT: 2 X KETTLEBELL
TARGET: BICEPS
INSTRUCTION:
1. STAND STRAIGHT AND GRAB KETTLEBELLS WITH MUG HOLD
2. BEND ELBOWS AND RAISE THE KETTLEBELL TOWARDS THE OPPOSITE CHEST SIDE
3. BACK TO THE START POSITION AND REPEAT ON THE OTHER SIDE

KNEE PRESS

LEVEL: MEDIUM

EQUIPMENT: 2 X KETTLEBELL

TARGET: BICEPS

INSTRUCTION:

1. GRAB KETTLEBELLS AND TAKE A SQUAT POSITION
2. PUT YOUR ELBOWS ON THE KNEES
3. LOW THE ELBOWS AND PULL THE KETTLEBELLS BACK
4. BACK TO THE START POSITION AND REPEAT

GUN PRESS

LEVEL: EASY

EQUIPMENT: 2 X KETTLEBELL

TARGET: BICEPS

INSTRUCTION:

1. STAND TALL AND GRAB KETTLEBELL WITH PISTOL GRIP

2. BEND THE ELBOW AND RAISE THE KETTLEBELLS UP

3. HOLD THE MOVE AND BACK TO THE START POSITION

BEND PRESS

LEVEL: EASY
EQUIPMENT: KETTLEBELL
TARGET: BICEPS
INSTRUCTION:
1. STAND STRAIGHT AND LOW YOUR POSITION
2. GRAB THE KETTLEBELL WITH ONE HAND WHILE THE OTHER ONE IS BASED ON THE THIGH
3. PRESS THE KETTLEBELL UP
4. REPEAT ON THE OTHER SIDE

ARM MUG BEND
LEVEL: EASY
EQUIPMENT: 2 X KETTLEBELL
TARGET: BICEPS
INSTRUCTION:
1. STAND STRAIGHT AND GRAB KETTLEBELL WITH MUG HOLD
2. BEND THE ELBOW AND PULL KETTLEBELLS UP
3. HOLD THE MOVE AND BACK TO THE START POSITION

NARROW GRIP PRESS

DIFFICULT LEVEL: EASY

EQUIPMENT: KETTLEBELL

WORK: BICEPS

INSTRUCTION:

1. STAND STRAIGHT AND GRAB THE UPSIDE DOWN KETTLEBELL HOLDER
2. BEND THE ELBOWS AND BRING THE KETTLEBELL UP
3. HOLD THE MOVE AND BACK TO THE START POSITION

 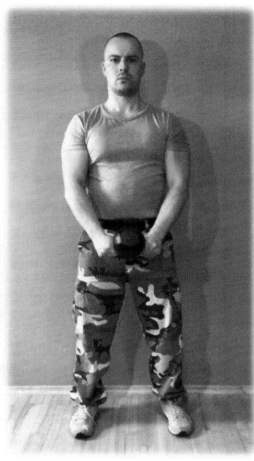

TRICEPS

TRICEP FLOOR PRESS
LEVEL: MEDIUM
EQUIPMENT: 2 X KETTLEBELL
TARGET: TRICPES
INSTRUCTION:
1. LAY ON THE FLOOR AND BEND THE KNEES
2. GRAB KETTLEBELLS AND PUSH THEM UP
3. BEND THE ELBOWS AND REPEAT

ONE ARM TRICEP FLOOR PRESS

LEVEL: MEDIUM
EQUIPMENT: 2 X KETTLEBELL
TARGET: TRICPES
INSTRUCTION:
1. LAY ON THE FLOOR AND BEND THE KNEES
2. GRAB KETTLEBELLS AND PUSH THEM UP
3. BEND YOUR ELBOW TO THE HEAD
4. REPEAT ON THE OTHER HAND

JUMPER SWING

LEVEL: EASY

EQUIPMENT: 2 X KETTLEBELL

TARGET: TRICEPS

INSTRUCTION:

1. STAND STRAIGHT AND BEND THE POSITION- STRAIGHT BACK AND THE POSITION OF THE SKI JUMPER

2. GRAB KETTLEBELLS AND PUSH THEM TOWARDS BACK

3. BACK TO THE START POSITION AND REPEAT

BEHING HEAD PRESS

LEVEL: EASY

EQUIPMENT: KETTLEBELL

TARGET: TRICEPS

INSTRUCTION:

1. LAY ON THE FLOOR AND BEND THE KNEES

2. GRAB THE KETTLEBELL AND LIFT ABOVE THE CHEST

3. BEND THE LEBOWS TOWARDS HEAD

3. GO BACK TO THE START POSITION AND REPEAT

ONE ARM STANDING PRESS
LEVEL: EASY
EQUIPMENT: KETTLEBELL
TARGET: TRICEPS
INSTRUCTION:
1. STAND STRAIGHT AND LIFT THE KETTLEBELL ABOVE HEAD
2. BEND THE ELBOW BEHIND THE HEAD
3. BACK TO START POSITION AND REPEAT

BOTH ARMS STANDING PRESS

LEVEL: MEDIUM

EQUIPMENT: KETTLEBELL

TARGET: TRICEPS

INSTRUCTION:

1. STAND STRAIGHT AND GRAB THE KETTLEBELL IN BOTH HANDS
2. LIFT THE KETTLEBELL ABOVE HEAD
3. BEND THE ELBOWS AND PUT KETTLEBELL BEHIND HEAD
4. BACK TO THE START POSITION AND REPEAT

FOREARMS

BENDING WRISTS
LEVEL: EASY
EQUIPMENT: KETTLEBELL
TARGET: FOREARM
INSTRUCTION:
1. STAND STRAIGHT AND GRAB THE KETTLEBELL HOLDER FACING YOUR SIDE
2. BEND THE WRISTS TO THE BODY SIDE
3. BACK TO START POSITION

REVERSE BENDING WRISTS

LEVEL: EASY

EQUIPMENT: KETTLEBELL

TARGET: TRICEPS

INSTRUCTION:

1. STAND STRAIGHT AND GRAB THE KETTLEBELL HOLDER FACING YOUR SIDE

2. BEND THE KETTLEBELL DOWN

3. BACK TO THE START POSITION AND REPEAT

FRONTAL BENDING

LEVEL: EASY

EQUIPMENT: KETTLEBELL

TARGET: FOREARM

INSTRUCTION:

1. STAND STRAIGHT AND GRAB THE KETTLEBELL

2. LIFT THE WRIST UP

3. BACK TO THE START POSITION AND REPEAT

BACK BENDING

LEVEL: EASY
EQUIPMENT: KETTLEBELL
TARGET: FOREARM
INSTRUCTION:
1. STAND STRAIGHT AND GRAB THE KETTLEBELL
2. LIFT THE WRIST DOWN
3. BACK TO THE START POSITION AND REPEAT

HIGH KETTLEBELL ROTATION

LEVEL: EASY

EQUIPMENT: KETTLEBELL

TARGET: FOREARM

INSTRUCTION:

1. STAND STRAIGHT AND GRAB THE KETTLEBELL – SHOULDERS HIGH

2. GRAB THE KETTLEBELL HOLDER AND ROTATE IT ALL THE WAY UP AND THEN DOWN

3. BACK TO THE START POSITION AND REPEAT

AROUND THE CLOCK
LEVEL: EASY
EQUIPMENT: KETTLEBELL
TARGET:FOREARM
INSTRUCTION:
1. STAND UP STRAIGHT AND GRAB THE KETTLEBELL IN FORNT OF YOU WITH BOTH HANDS
2. MAKE A ROATTE MOVE BEHIND THE BACK
3. PASS THE KETTLEBELL TO THE OTHER HAND NAD ROATTE IT BACK TO THE FRONTAL POSITION
4. REPEAT ON THE OTHER SIDE

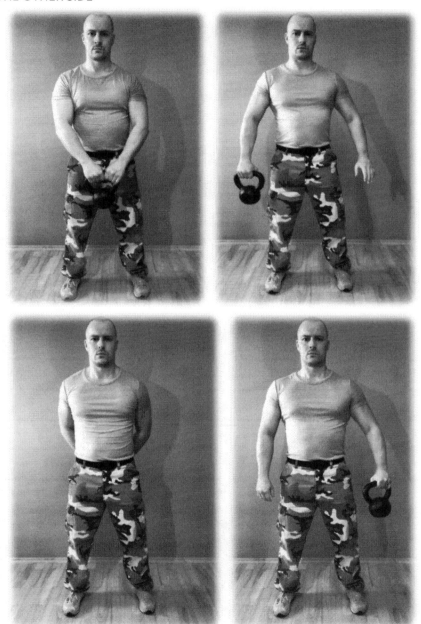

FULL BODY WORKOUT

• Weight, number of repetitions, number of sets and all components depend on the individual training plan and training goal.

1. CLOCK
2. EIGHT
3. DEADLIFT
4. PULLING UP
5. SWING
6. SQUAT
7. PUSH UPS
8. BENDING ARMS
9. TRICEPS
10. HALO

WWW.DROGASKORPIONA.COM

Made in the USA
Las Vegas, NV
22 October 2024